Just Before, Immediately After.
Instants of an Architecture in Motion
Nina Bassoli

There is a moment, at dawn, when all the colours that begin to break through the darkness – first the deepest blue, then the dusty violet, the pale blue, the pyrite pink, the faint almost greenish yellow, … – meet for an instant and illuminate the sky. At that precise moment, just before the day comes, light is made up of the sum of all colours and the sky is, for a sudden instant, absolutely white. Dante describes this moment at the beginning of Purgatory (Dante Alighieri, *The Divine Comedy*, *II*, Canto 2) as a kind of premonition, but also a very natural, everyday phenomenon.

In addition to its beauty, that moment contains the enchantment of its fragility: a single fleeting instant in which the sky appears empty, just before being once again filled with all the increasingly brazen colours brought by dawn at the gates of day. A moment of breath, suspension.

It is here that Rory Gardiner reveals the Garden House. It appears, like a mirage suspended between night and day, like an unexpected concrete figure of an unrepeatable moment.

All the colours are already there, yet still suspended, ready to go, as if waiting.

In a few seconds, the light will begin to cast its coloured reflections on the panes, the sky will start to turn pink, orange, red, then gradually purple and finally sky blue, and the inhabitants will start to wake up, filling it in turn with their own colours, movements and activities.

Vegetation will never look like this again; only one minute before, the soil, its herbaceous inhabitants and the insects were younger, and one minute later they will be a little bit riper.

I don't believe it is by chance that Gardiner chose this peculiar moment for shooting pictures of the Garden House. As a photographer who grew up in the world of fashion, he looks at the ephemeral as a fundamental trace of reality, he looks for the moment, and likewise he looks at architecture starting from its position in time, even before than in space.

The house, in turn, is conceived as a non-stable architecture: it is a provisional shelter – Mauro Baracco and Louise Wright talk about something "a little more than a tent", breathing, growing, moving symbiotically with the environment in which it is immersed. Here, the borders between interior and exterior are fleeting and the natural ground creeps seamlessly into the living spaces as much as into the domestic outdoor terraces and the surrounding wilderness, demonstrating that architecture does not necessarily have to be an interruption of the living humus covering the earth, but rather defending a 'spatial continuity' of coexistence between all beings.

Rory Gardiner captures this concept, the manifesto, in a sense, of Baracco+Wright's entire work, with some peculiar moves that are anything but accidental, presenting the house as a mirror of his philosophy.

1. On the threshold

If the house expresses a desire for 'spatial continuity', Gardiner's work transposes this idea onto the temporal plane, capturing its 'continuity' in time. The photographer's eye always stands on a threshold, the threshold between inside and outside, between night and day, to convey an idea of synchronicity. Hence the sweet but also uncanny sense of expectation given by the muted colour of dawn: after night, before day; closer than the forest, further than the interior.

Often, when looking at the pictures, we can't tell whether we are looking from inside to outside or from outside to inside. Vegetation grows indiscriminately on either side of the vertical surfaces. The polycarbonate sheets are not partition walls, but elements that cooperate with the environment, similar to theatrical backdrops, which orient the actors' movements. Some ordinary elements indicate that life takes place outside and inside the house. Gardiner includes them in the images without any particular accent, but adding to the suspended atmosphere a narrative touch. Did something just happen? Is something going to happen?

Everyday objects indicate the extent of the borderless space and focus the attention revealing the 'punctum' of the images.

In the first image of the sequence, a few signs emerge from the woodland scrub: the metal profiles of the structure stand out against the sky and in the foreground, two barely visible sinuous lines lie on the ground. A closer look reveals they are two deckchairs without their seats, generously made available for the use of other inhabitants, an idea not too far from that of the house itself. Here too, in fact, some functional elements are missing, and the structure is left free for anyone to use. No sealed closures, no separating edges, or, eventually, the architecture is seen as an edge itself. The steel and polycarbonate structure recalls agricultural equipment, but a graceful lamp suspended in the air brings the space back to a domestic dimension. The kitchen top looks like an abstract white line stretched across the bush, but the freshly washed dishes resting on the counter indicate the real nature of the place: this is a room, where some human being has eaten and cleaned up. So, what is

2

1

3

a room? – the photographs seem to ask. Is it a space enclosed by four walls? Or is it rather, simply, a place where someone performs certain activities?

We can clearly recognise in these questions the debt of Baracco+Wright to the thought of Martin Heidegger, amply argued in their writings, as in their stunning reading of Robin Boyd's architecture (see Mauro Baracco and Louise Wright, *Robin Boyd: Spatial Continuity*, Routledge, 2017). In fact, if man can inhabit even 'before' architecture, as the German philosopher argues in his famous conference *Building Dwelling Thinking* (Darmstadt, 1951), the limit separating the habitable from the uninhabitable falls away, and we can let trees grow in the bedroom and sleep in a veranda, calling all this 'home'.

2. Out of focus. A gaze from within

Another paradigm shift marked by Baracco+Wright's architecture can be detected starting from the use of light in Gardiner's photographs. Indeed, Le Corbusier's renowned statement according to which architecture is "the masterly, correct and magnificent play of masses brought together in light" no longer seems relevant for this type of architecture. If we were used to look at architecture as a sum of capturing light surfaces, in Gardiner's pictures architecture seems rather to radiate light, acting not as an obstacle but as an amplifier. He is careful to avoid any possibility of drawing sharp shadows, and instead lets the light penetrate from behind, filling the entire picture with a kind of solid, coherent atmosphere with no precise direction. From whatever perspective Gardiner frames the house, he never brings it in as a central presence, but rather tends to dissolve its materiality.

Gardiner's attention to the perception around the field of view in photography is anything but unconscious and involves the technical and psychological spectres of the photographic media. The human eye sees at 49.2mm (35mm equivalent) which is known as the approximate standard field of view; every deviation from this standard elicits a different subconscious response, he explains: there is a continuum in both directions. Traditional architecture photography typically relies on

4

5

extremely wide fields of view to illustrate a project in its entirety. In Gardiner's own words: "I think this 'entirety' of a project is more interestingly explored through subtle deviations from the standard field of view. Erring just to the wider side of a standard can evoke a sense of calmness and the ability to look without the violence of an attempt to represent the whole. Conversely, images just slightly further compressed than 49.2mm offer an intimacy less common in architecture – a way to explore the entirety in the abstract or gentle nod to human peripheral vision that photography will never truthfully translate".

This way of photographing denies all forms of planning also in the choice of the viewpoint, and thus somehow even denies the ego of the shooting eye in favor of an immersive gaze. The photographer finds himself working from the inside, from within the space, as in a continuum of strata and sensations. What emerges in the picture is not a space structured around a vanishing point, but rather a whole blurring entity, which radiates through superimposing layers. Material layers – the polycarbonate, the steel, the wood of the construction – ; atmospheric layers, where the many colours of light appear in a fog like in a Mark Rothko painting; and, finally, the layers of life, of human and non-human traces, of the passage of time, blending into an image with no vanishing point. The effect is that of a gradual appearance of reality, echoed in the intentions of the project, which is itself meant to be programmatically incomplete until the vegetation and other species will gradually start to inhabit the space.

3. A non-hegemonic perspective. From architecture to landscape

This also means, in a very radical way, the will to remove from the images the idea of the perspective point of view from which everything originates. The presumption of an alleged objectivity of the gaze is deposed: photography attempts to see things piece by piece, not to take them apart, but to recompose them. It is a way of knowing, fragment by fragment, enunciating the whole.

Gardiner's background as a non-architectural photographer is related with this approach: "my way of working is very intuitive. I am not an architectural literate, my dad was an architect, but I would never know how to talk about a detail of architecture, and I don't even really care that much. I think I have a completely different experience of architecture. It is much more about a bigger picture, the sensations, the feeling you get when you enter a space. That puts me in the position of an ordinary person and can make me perceive different things: I can find an interesting imperfection, something that an architect would never want to see. Fashion has been very important in pushing me to let go until I get the essence of a project, rather than literally documenting it with details, etc."

Rory Gardiner's work is based on a 'responsive' attitude, which accepts reality as it is, in order to let all the more subtle elements of the context enter the visual field little by little.

Far from the conceptual approach of the German photographers from the Dusseldorf School, Gardiner seems to refer to another photographic tradition, less structured but no less significant, linked to the artistic and architectural context of the last decades of the 20th century in Italy, not by chance Mauro Baracco's homeland. Here, photographers such as Luigi Ghirri and Guido Guidi, and later Vincenzo Castella, Gabriele Basilico and Giovanni Chiaramonte, contributed significantly to broaden the field of vision in architectural photography. Vincenzo Castella explains very well the period mood in an interview released to Pierluigi Nicolin in the pages of *Lotus international* magazine: "Luigi's time was different, then there was the hypothesis of representation, representation with our experience... Essentially it signified the transposition of an almost theatrical attitude. In fact even then it was contrasted with the attitude of journalistic investigation supposedly linked to truth, to the relation with reality. ...And in all this was included as principal attitude the relationship with architecture. It is no accident that Ghirri, Chiaramonte, myself and Basilico have to all intents and purposes photographed architecture, works of architecture, and not the nude. Why architecture? A series – for me principally – a series of empty boxes to be filled with memory" (Pierluigi Nicolin, 'Architecture and Photography: Three Histories. The Influence of Photography on Architecture', *Lotus international*, no. 129, *Photographs*, 2006, p. 8). In turning to architecture, as if places were simply waiting for someone to look at them or to recognise them, the extraordinary work of those photographers who have shifted their gaze from architecture to landscape begins, constructing a cartography that is "imprecise, without cardinal points, which is concerned more with the perception of a place than with its cataloguing or description" (ibid.).

With their eyes, those photographers help to shift the gaze of architects themselves and to reallocate architecture and buildings into a wider horizon, able to include unplanned traces and, as mentioned before, different layers of life.

Guido Guidi, much loved by Gardiner, never moved from his home district, just outside Cesena, a small town in north-eastern Italy between Rimini and Bologna. He spent a large part of his life walking around the same streets, looking and looking at the same things, often shooting the same photo in different moments of the day. Appointed to photograph Carlo Scarpa's Brion Cemetery, in the province of Treviso, northern Italy, he describes his work as a sequence of waiting moments, in search of an ephemeral form produced for instance by the shadows on the concrete walls in a precise moment in time. In the end, Guidi's beautiful shots show the same framing of the wall in the water, where a wire passes through some pulleys to hold up an object, producing three different triangles of shadow. "I was taking a collective photo and, by chance, just before one o'clock, I began to follow this shadow as it moved. The parallelogram of light from the square above moved along the adjacent wall and, given that there is a corner of the chapel that points exactly north, at midday (solar time)

6

it made a triangle... I tried to see how a triangle is deformed and to photograph the transformation in time and light... In many of the spaces in this place I have found geometries and marks that compose arrows. It is the image of transformation through time", Guidi reports (Guido Guidi, *Lotus international*, no. 129, *Photographs*, 2006, pp. 12-15).

Returning to Gardiner's photographs, it comes to mind the only photo in which a person is visible, if only for a small fragment: the candid image of the unmade bed in which a lock of hair emerges from the duvet. Nothing is happening: the girl is asleep, as just before and as immediately after; everything is still. And yet, at that very moment, the light and all the other inhabitants of the place are moving; architecture, too, is imperceptibly moving. There is no vanishing point, no 'decisive moment', but a sequence of 'provisional moments'. The photographer has put his ego aside, and so did the architect: no stable form, but rather the "masterly, correct and magnificent play" of coexisting things brought together in life.

1   Guido Guidi, *September 11, 2003, about midday*, San Vito di Altivole, 2003.
    Carlo Scarpa, Brion Cemetery. Copyright ©Guido Guidi-CISA A. Palladio
2   Ibid.
3   Ibid.
4   Luigi Ghirri, Lame di Fasano, 1986. Copyright ©Eredi di Luigi Ghirri
5   Giovanni Chiaramonte, *A Vision of the Modern*, Rio de Janeiro, 2005.
    Oscar Niemeyer, Casas das Canoas
6   Rory Gardiner, Jaffna, Asia. 2011

Garden House
Baracco+Wright Architects

Lecture transcript, delivered by Mauro Baracco and Louise Wright at *The Hybrid House - Design Speaks symposium*, Daylesford, Australia, 26 February 2022

1. Buildings and Living Things

2. In its most simple description, this house is a hybrid between a building and living things.

3. The building's siting, materiality and spatial conditions are in a large part defined by other species that the house would have displaced,

4. plants mostly, and what is required to sustain them such as deep soil, light and connectivity.

5. A house, a garden. A garden house.

6. A garden is tended/manipulated/artificial…but maybe more accurately in relation to a garden house is the etymology of the word 'gardening' that refers to 'enclosure': it is from Middle English 'garden', from Anglo-French 'gardin', 'jardin', of Germanic origin; akin to Old High German 'gard', 'gart', meaning: an enclosure or compound.

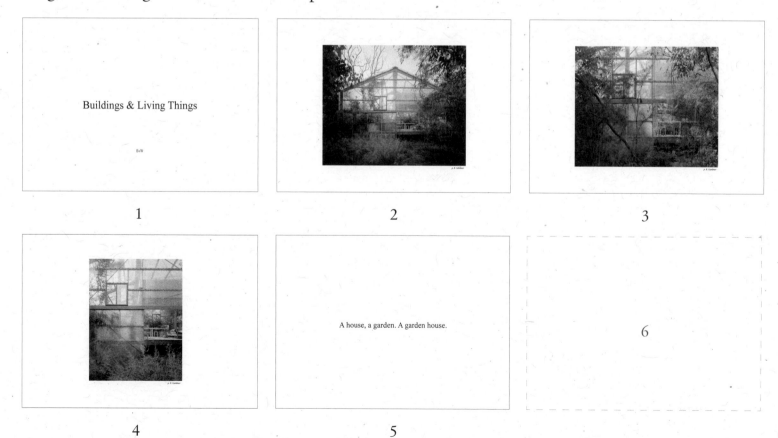

1   2   3

4   5

Context plan

1. Melbourne
2. House
3. Port Phillip Bay
4. Westernport
5. French Island
6. Phillip Island
7. Southern Ocean

North south section

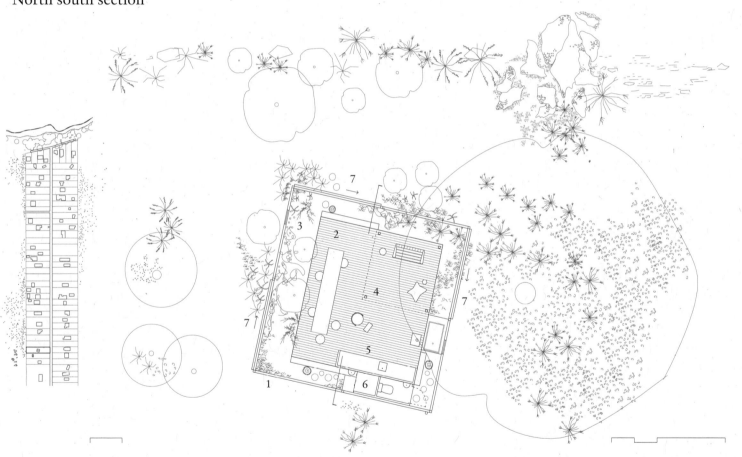

Site plan

Plan

1. Kit shed enclosure
2. Raised deck
3. Garden
4. Mezzanine over
5. Kitchen
6. Shower, wc
7. Sliding doors

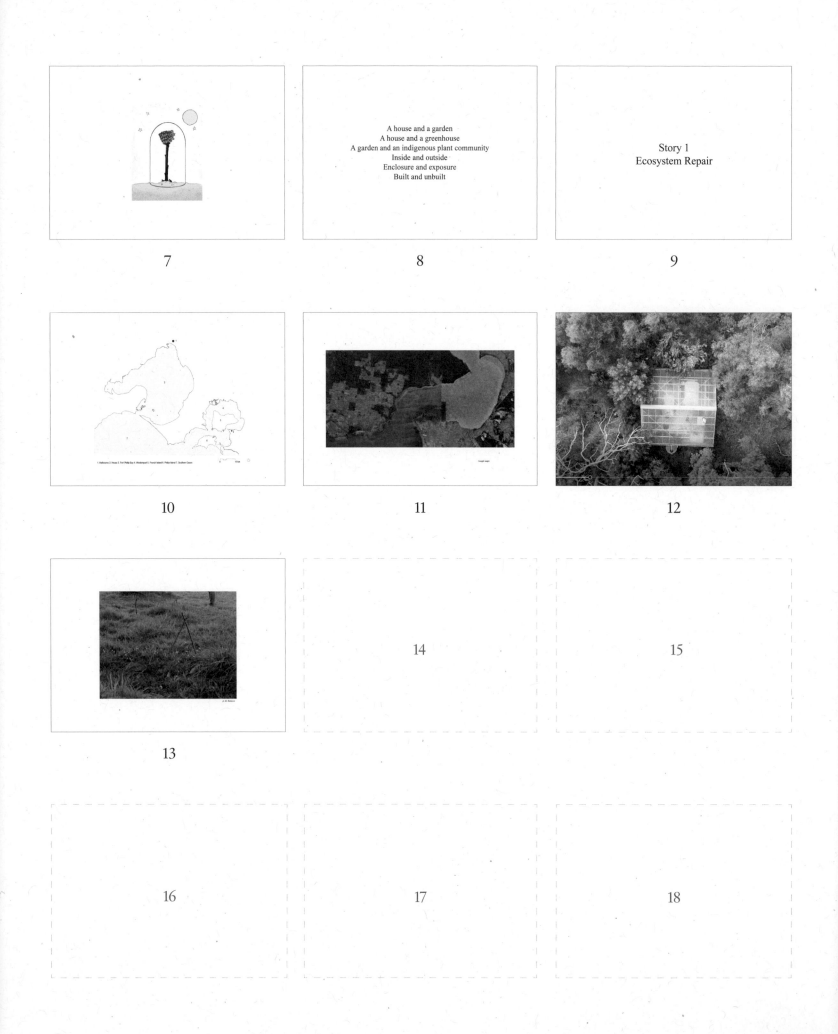

7

A house and a garden
A house and a greenhouse
A garden and an indigenous plant community
Inside and outside
Enclosure and exposure
Built and unbuilt

8

Story 1
Ecosystem Repair

9

10

11

12

13

14

15

16

17

18

7. The glass jar over the Little Prince's rose comes to mind.

   You could also say it is:

8. A house and a greenhouse
   A garden and an indigenous plant community
   Inside and outside
   Enclosure and exposure
   Built and unbuilt

   In the unpacking of these hybrids are multiple stories that occupy our work and thought.

9. *Story 1: Ecosystem Repair*

   This is the most instructive place to start, and how the house came to be how it is.

   Observation of the natural history of the site drove much of the decision making.

10. The site, Boon Wurrung country, connects to its neighbouring vegetation and Westernport –
    a large tidal bay of international ecological significance.

11. The site is part of a leftover heavily vegetated corridor in between cleared grazing land. A
    historical anomaly, it gives a glimpse into what used to be there, although it too now is mostly
    altered through domestic gardens, humans and their animals. This strip is part of a larger modified
    system that acts as a compromised wildlife corridor for animals travelling from nearby Gurdies
    Nature Conservation Reserve to the coast, and perhaps most successfully supports birds.

12. In this drone footage, *Above*, 2021, by Paulina Cur

    [*Play*]

    we see the site undergoing repair, small patches of the endemic vegetation remained, mainly
    Tea-tree Heath, among mown grass, introduced species and plants considered invasive weeds.
    We see the surrounding mowed and grazed grass, which is what this site was like 10 years ago.

    [*Stop*]

13. The existence of endemic terrestrial orchids indicated that the soil had not been altered, and
    that, embedded in the soil and under the introduced grass were the bones of a plant community
    that once grew there.

14. -235 years, Boon Wurrung Country.

15. -60 years, Boon Wurrung Country:
    -60 to -10 years, road sealed, pasture
    grass invades indigenous vegetation,
    trees cleared, buildings and subdivision,
    domestic dogs and cats introduced.

16. 0 years, Boon Wurrung Country:
    weeding continued, indigenous species
    continue to emerge over 50 species
    recorded not present 10 years ago.

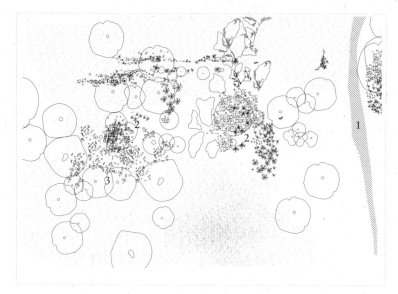

14

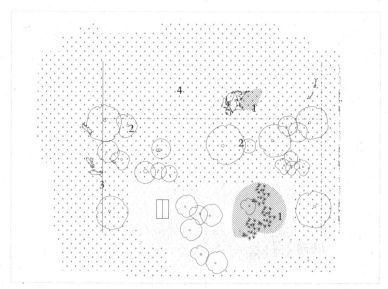

15

1. Ephemeral water
2. Tea-tree Heath
3. Seasonal orchids + lillies
4. Pasture grass, cleared land
5. Garden house
6. Revegetation
7. Flood zone

16

14. In these diagrams we trace the site's recent past. The road now occupies the position of an ephemeral creek, and being downhill, the area can be seasonally wet and dry, and can flood.

15. With an aim to support the strength of the remnant indigenous vegetation present on the site, weeding was carried out using the Bradley method: which works from any small patch of remnant outward, so that slowly the vegetation can re-establish. What is occurring is a new type of balance supported by us, at least for now.

16. By observing and supporting the expansion of small remnant patches of endemic vegetation, a shape of the site emerged that revealed ephemeral water as well as an area where no regeneration was occurring, and as it turned out had been the site of imported fill, effectively smothering the seed stock and altering the soil.

17. We situated the house on this 'clearing' – here we see the complete structure as if a big tent.

18. It is raised above the ground to allow for overland flow and so as not to 'cut' the site. Apart from a small utilities area, no ground is sealed. This supports the expansion of the vegetation inside the house.

17   18

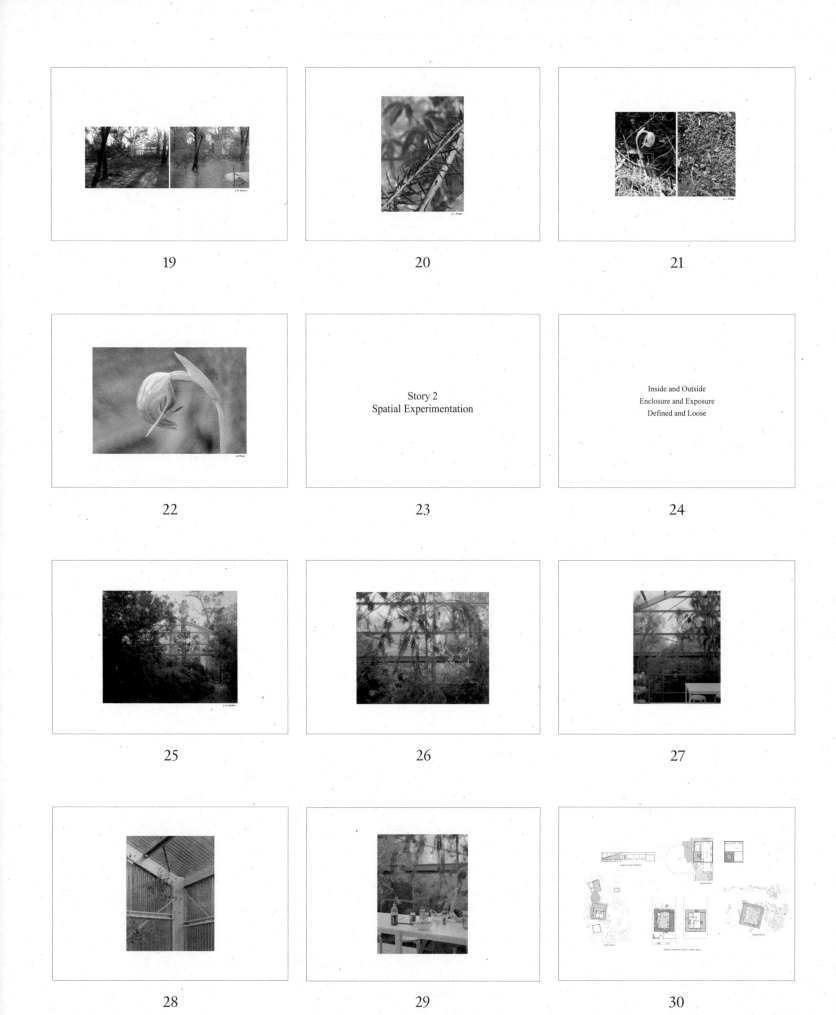

19

20

21

22

23
Story 2
Spatial Experimentation

24
Inside and Outside
Enclosure and Exposure
Defined and Loose

25

26

27

28

29

30

19. Now part of this ecosystem, this house supports life. The disturbance generated by the construction was quite minimal, but nonetheless enough to generate the expansion of tea trees (which respond to disturbance),

20. … and they now regularly grow inside in their turn supporting other life, like this praying mantis.

    Fragmented from the overall web of relationships and natural systems, it is difficult to know if this ongoing activity is strengthening a plant community or if it will now always depend on human care.

21. The presence of Nodding Greenhood orchids (*Pterostylis nutans*) is evidence of the presence of *Mycorrhizae* (required at the germination stage) and often a symbiotic relationship with certain trees. *Mycorrhizal* fungi is a crucial foundation for healthy soils and have recently been credited with the network used by trees to communicate with each other.

22. Continued mowing and fertilisation of the (introduced) grass on the site when it was bought, a hasty positioning of the house on their location, potential changes to the hydrology of the site such as water penetration and overland flow, and symbiotic tree removal among other disturbances would have meant these orchids would have disappeared in the near future.

23. *Story 2: Spatial Experimentation*

24. Inside and Outside
    Enclosure and Exposure
    Defined and Loose

25. An ongoing occupation in our office are veranda-type spaces.

26. In their looseness we find informality, flexibility and delight.

27. We also wonder about the reimagining of an architecture that is spatially continuous, ground and roof, or ill-defined in its threshold with 'outside', we wonder about phenomenological notions of space closer to Indigenous First Nations peoples being in the world not on it…

28. [*Pause*]

29. The veranda is the ontological opening for architecture, as if under a tree…

30. In the spatial quality of our work the loose or veranda space can be traced. The tent and veranda have often been a reference for us and this building could be thought as a little more than a tent:

31. a deck and raised platform, covered by a transparent 'shed', the interior perimeter 'veranda' this time is vegetation, and living areas are

32. dynamic yet subtly spatially defined; up, down, under, above.

33. This arrangement, or non-arrangement of overlapping domestic spaces is what the hybrid asks of the house.

34. [*Pause*]

35. [*Pause*]

36. The spatial boundaries are not achieved in usual architectural terms (walls, windows, and rooms, ceiling and floor)

31

32

33

34

35

36

37. but made by the vegetation on either side of the polycarbonate layer,

38. not perhaps quite a wall,

39. but together with the vegetation an ill-defined wall is made that starts on

40. the inside with the moat-like horizontal boundary achieved through the way the raised floor stops

41. short of the polycarbonate.

42. The raised deck is another expanded threshold, this time with the ground,

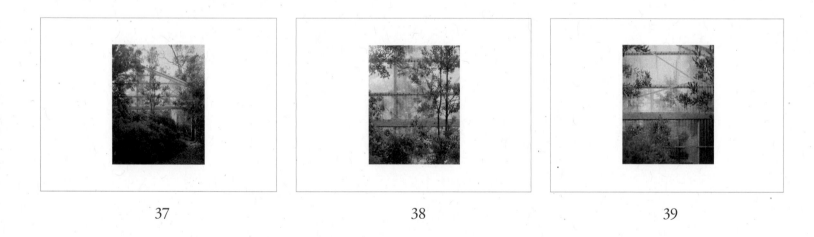

37   38   39

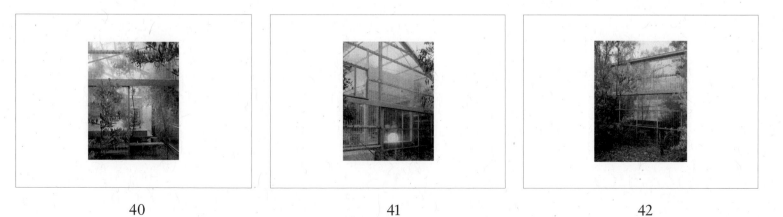

40   41   42

43. allowing the unsealed ground and its floodwaters to carry through.

44. [*Pause*]

45. [*Pause*]

46. [*Pause*]

47. The window that frames an interior's relationship with nature is absent.

48. Nature is neither confined to containers or *brought* inside.

49. This quality of space is evident in Rory Gardiner's photographic technique where

50. frames are often replaced by images that fill the view without edges,

51. so that it is sometimes unclear if you are looking from *inside* or *outside*. In reflecting on ideas of 'spatial continuity' we acknowledge an Indigenous worldview.

52. We recently had the privilege

53. to interview indigenous spatial designer Danièle Hromek, a Budawang woman of the Yuin nation.

54. We offer a small moment of the transcript accompanied by Linda Tegg and David Fox's 2-channel video of Garden House made for *Repair* at the Australian Pavilion, at the 2018 Venice Architecture Biennale. Each of the 14 videos are filmed from two points of view to disrupt the architectural concepts of façade, object, front and back, and instead privilege the spatial continuity.

55. From *Ground* video series – [*Play video from 1.18 minute*]

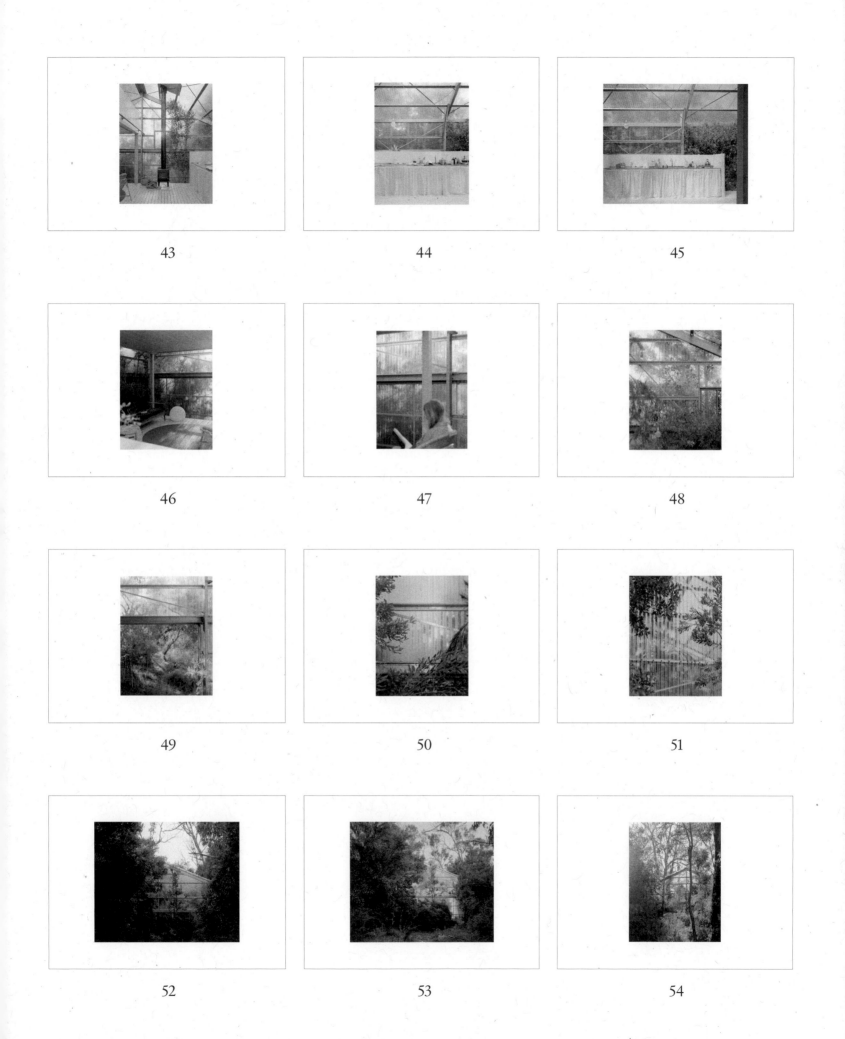

43

44

45

46

47

48

49

50

51

52

53

54

0:00:05

0:05:23

30

Louise: "I'm myself"

Mauro: "I'm Danièle"

[*Pause*]

LW: Could you speak more to Aboriginal (or your) peoples' spatial values? Does the concept of void exist in your Indigenous thinking? (sorry if these questions are too ridiculously huge…)

DH: Of course. Space is *held* by Country. Let's think about this some more. If Country holds space, then space, by its very nature, is full of Country. Country is not only the land, water and sky and the tangible elements we can see or touch, it is also the intangible, the relationships, knowledges, values, etc. More than this, it is the potential for everything. Country, holding space, is potentiality, or the opposite of what is often understood to be a void. Spaces also hold values. So this might be, for instance, values understood through cultural practices, however the values might also be gendered or intergenerational or narrational. In fact, without the story, it is pretty hard to make sense. Of anything.

Back to the Garden House…

The fabric and shelter of houseness is tenuous, in the temperate south-eastern Australian climate, one is sometimes a little cold and a little hot but mostly comfortable under the trees.

[*Stop video at 4.18 minute*]

56. *Story 3: Typological*

57. Architecture Sharing Space, Built and Unbuilt

58. Architecture's physicality is its problem but also its potential way forward in its relationship with its site and the species supported there. Its physical size, shape, footprint and material allow it to 'make', share, or release ground.

Possibilities include admitting light, being a life supporting substrate or structure and creating ground through verticality, reducing the need to take up land and displace life elsewhere.

Seemingly simple, by reframing how we know these approaches as one of sharing. For architecture to share these few metres above and below the surface of the ground is difficult and requires compromise on both parts in a play of light, shade, wind, water, noise, access and importantly flux. Garden House is an experiment in sharing which we are learning from.

The typological experiments of building and site take many forms which we can briefly describe some examples of here to give you a sense of what we mean.

59. Rearranging

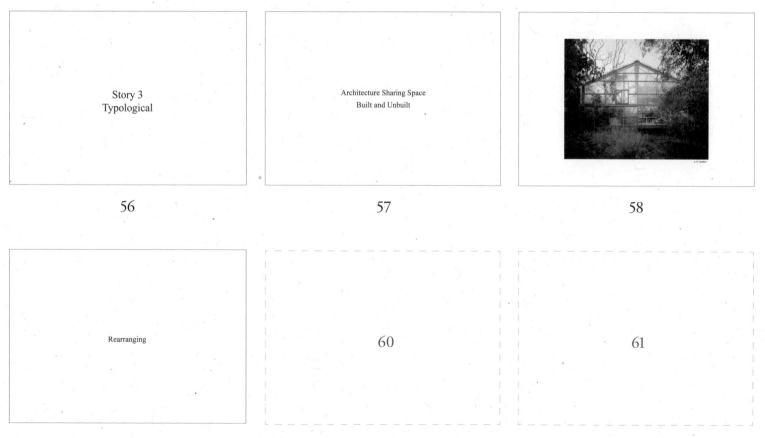

Story 3
Typological

56

Architecture Sharing Space
Built and Unbuilt

57

58

Rearranging

59

60

61

Forte Giaura   p. M. Baracco

60

Forte Pernante   p. M. Baracco

60. Architecture has long been made by moving around what is on a site, or Country, to form a new arrangement that suits the need at hand: here, in rearranging the stone and soil of the Maritime Alps on the Italian-French border between the Roya Valley and Vermenagna Valley. Built in the 19th century, but once finished hardly used, a chain of six forts span altitudes from 1850 to 2270m above sea level: Forte Colle Alto, Margheria, Taborda, Pernante, Pepino and Giaura, depicted in this photo. Giaura is the most embedded of all forts. With a pentagonal plan it remakes a hilltop: an architecture made by removing (to create the moat-like threshold) and relocating soil to the 'roof' so that it is grassed and completes the hill.

61. In the moat – an architectural element all forts were provided with (here we see the one of the Forte Pernante) – a microclimate forms, protected from the high-altitude winds, and now site of a new ecosystem. This roof, like the roofs of all six forts, is a functioning *ground* with soil and depth. It reminds any architect of a certain age of the excitement of

62. Paul Virilio's *Bunker Archeology* and the revelation that architecture can be found in unlikely combinations of mass and bulk in geological forms and 'allowed' to sink into their sites.

63. Acknowledging their military past, there is something once reframed about these architectures, the undeniable mass yet lightness at the same time – being there yet not there – is the architectural reality of trying to look like a mountain – of being the mountain.

64. Reusing

In a contemporary application of using material at hand – the 21st century project of architecture might well be the reuse of what we have already made (with the 22nd being the removal of what we don't need anymore) – we can reimagine architecture's relationships, and the whole concept of urban could break down.

62   63   64

65. We would like to think reuse is the future of architecture. Here we see the reuse of a toilet block, into a community centre (Weave Youth and Community Services, Collins and Turner, Sydney, 2013), the simple act of less waste, less extraction and less land used is made. At the same time this hybrid building brings a shared space for species above itself in the tree canopy-like structure that supports multiple plant species and forms habitat.

66. Taking up the ground displaces the systems that act in and through the surface and just above and just below it. In this architecture the space 5 metres above the ground is still somewhat connected.

67. Making 'ground'

68. Reframing our point of view, the high-rise apartment tower, is the most unlikely yet powerful gift of architecture and its capacity to make its own ground in the simple fact that it does not otherwise take up land contained there. Acknowledging the resources extracted for its construction, the hole that is somewhere far away is perhaps something to bring into one's mind and work on. When this typology is coupled with a large open vegetated space this potential is potent – *here goes the land we would have used*. In 1962, 20 additional grounds (around 10.000m^2, the equivalent of 1 hectare) were made in the sky in one of Melbourne's first high-rise apartment buildings (Domain Towers, Robin Boyd, 1962) across from the Royal Botanic Gardens (38 hectares).

69. Common to these architectures, at times only available in their reframing, is their being *of* the world – *with the world* as Donna Haraway would say –

Weave Youth and Community Services, Collins and Turner   p.S. Vogt

p.S. Vogt

Making 'ground'

65   66   67

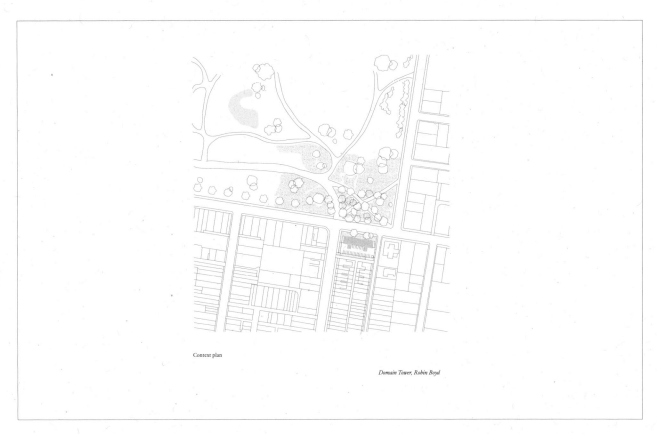

Context plan

Domain Tower, Robin Boyd

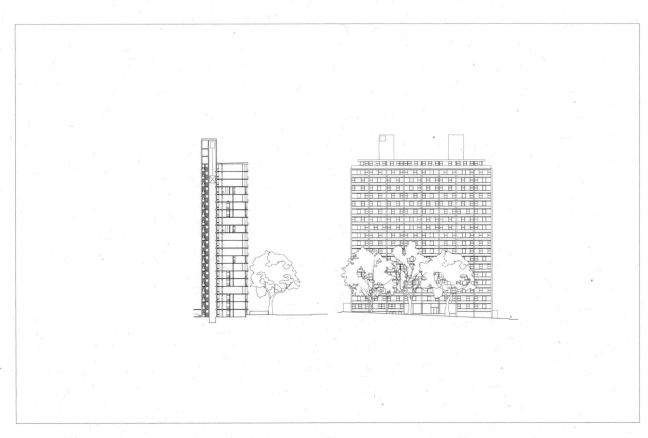

70. most potently in their spatial continuity, and so, requiring a considered relationship with their site, the ground, and inherently the species supported there.

71. Traversing

72. Shinohara describes the Tanikawa House (Kazuo Shinohara, 1972-1974, Nagano, Japan) as giving form to the 'gap' which opened up between the raw slope and the structure of the house,

73. and an interest in discovering an 'anti-space'. It follows from his House with an Earthern Floor (1963) and House of Earth (1966) and before his essay "When Naked Space is Traversed".

74. The concept of traversing inherently shifts the point of view to that being traversed,

75. that is the ground, as the focus of the architecture.

[*Pause*]

76. At the Garden House we have recently been making holes in the roof to allow the trees and plants inside to get out, and have started to accept that in time we might have to leave it.

70

Traversing

71

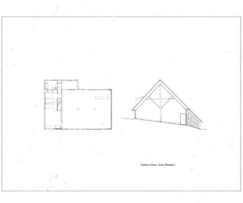

72

73

74

75

Biographies

Rory Gardiner is an Australian photographer working primarily between the UK, Switzerland, Mexico and Australia. Collaborating with architects, his work inhabits the space where contemporary photography and architecture intersect, adding a layer of authorship to the human experience of the built environment. His images interrogate architectural vernaculars, the structure of landscape and the objects populating the spaces he photographs. Working primarily through traditional analogue processes, Rory also experiments with motion and computer generated components.

Nina Bassoli is an architect, researcher and curator, since 2022 coordinator of the Architecture, Urban Regeneration, City sector at the Triennale di Milano. Nina Bassoli has a PhD from IUAV Venice, and studied at Milan Polytechnic, where she teaches Architectural Design. She taught at UTPL in Loja, Ecuador and held the research grant *Architecture in the Age of Display*, at the Free University in Bolzano (2019-2021). Since 2008 Nina has been a member of *Lotus international* editorial staff, and curator of several exhibitions – among others: *Reconstructions* (Triennale di Milano 2018), *Architecture as Art* (Pirelli HangarBicocca Milano 2018), *ADI. Take your Seat* (Supersalone Milano 2020).

Louise Wright and Mauro Baracco, architects, both PhD, are directors of Baracco+Wright Architects (B+W, est. 2004) and their research laboratory B+W+. They both teach and research. Mauro was an Associate Professor at RMIT (1996-2020) and Louise is a Practice Professor at MADA (Monash Art Design & Architecture) Monash University. Their interest in the local has developed from historical and cultural to include ecological relationships of the built and unbuilt environment. They are interested in a role for architecture that can extend its relationship with the natural world towards one that considers all life. They build, unbuild, rearrange and support buildings and living things. Recently they have been researching the role of reuse and removal of built form in the reimagining of the city.

Credits

pp. 1-37, *Garden House*, 2014-ongoing, Baracco+Wright Architects, photos Rory Gardiner

p. 40, *September 11, 2003, about midday*, San Vito di Altivole, 2003. Carlo Scarpa, Brion Cemetery, photos Guido Guidi. Copyright ©Guido Guidi-CISA A. Palladio

p. 41, no. 4, Lame di Fasano, 1986, photo Luigi Ghirri. Copyright ©Eredi di Luigi Ghirri

p. 41, no. 5, *A Vision of the Modern*, Rio de Janeiro, 2005. Oscar Niemeyer, Casas das Canoas, photo Giovanni Chiaramonte

p. 44, Jaffna, Asia, 2011, photo Rory Gardiner

pp. 47-69, slides from 'Garden House: Lecture Transcript', 26.02.2022, Baracco+Wright Architects

p. 50, slide no. 12, screen capture of *Above*, 2021, Paulina Cur

pp. 60-61, screen capture of *Ground,* 2018, Linda Tegg and David Fox with Baracco+Wright Architects

Supporters

This book was made possible in part with the generous support of the School of Architecture and Urban Design-RMIT University, and Ampelite Australia.

Title
Buildings & Living Things: Garden House

Published by
Actar Publishers, New York, Barcelona
www.actar.com

Authors
Louise Wright and Mauro Baracco, Baracco+Wright Architects

Typesetting
Arabella Kilmartin

With contributions by
Rory Gardiner, Nina Bassoli

Printing and binding
DZA Druckerei zu Altenburg GmbH

Distribution
Actar D, Inc. New York, Barcelona.

New York
440 Park Avenue South, 17th Floor
New York, NY 10016, USA
T +1 2129662207
salesnewyork@actar-d.com

Barcelona
Roca i Batlle 2-4
08023 Barcelona, Spain
T +34 933 282 183
eurosales@actar-d.com

Indexing
English ISBN: 978-1-94876-580-0
Library of Congress Control Number: 2022940445

Printed in Germany

Publication date: May 2023

Number Two, 2023

Louise and Mauro acknowledge the people of the Kulin Nation as the
traditional custodians of the land upon which they work and live. They in
particular acknowledge the Boon Wurrung and Bunurong people as the
traditional owners and custodians of the land upon which the Garden
House and the ongoing project of environmental repair are located,
acknowledging as well all the species that have been displaced.

Louise and Mauro would like to thank the contributors Nina and Rory
and those whose work appears in the lecture transcript, particularly
Linda Tegg and David Fox. Thank you also to Guido Guidi, Giovanni
Chiaramonte, Archivio Ghirri, and Guido Beltramini and Elisabetta
Michelato of Centro internazionale di studi di architettura Andrea
Palladio (CISA A. Palladio). Thank you very much to David Fox who
came through at the 11th hour.

Thank you to the School of Architecture and Urban Design-RMIT
University and Ampelite Australia for their generous support.